WOOD CARVING

BOY SCOUTS OF AMERICA
IRVING, TEXAS

Requirements

1. Show that you know first aid for injuries or illnesses that could occur while wood carving, including minor cuts and scratches and splinters.

2. Do the following:
   a. Earn the Totin' Chip recognition.
   b. Discuss with your merit badge counselor your understanding of the Safety Checklist for Carving.

3. Do the following:
   a. Explain to your counselor, orally or in writing, the care and use of five types of tools that you may use in a carving project.
   b. Tell your counselor how to care for and use several types of sharpening devices, then demonstrate that you know how to use these devices.

4. Using a piece of scrap wood or a project on which you are working, show your merit badge counselor that you know how to do the following:
   a. Paring cut
   b. Basic cut and push cut
   c. Score line
   d. Stop cut

5. Tell why different woods are used for different projects. Explain why you chose the type of wood you did for your projects in requirements 6 and 7.

6. Plan your own or select a project from this merit badge pamphlet and complete a simple carving in the round.

7. Complete a simple low-relief OR a chip carving project.

33309A
ISBN 0-8395-3309-8
©2001 Boy Scouts of America
2004 Printing

Contents

Introduction

Wood carving can be an enjoyable hobby and lifetime activity. Making things with your hands can be very satisfying. If you like the idea of whittling and think you would like to earn the Wood Carving merit badge, you should know that there is more to wood carving than being a fair-to-middling whittler.

What is the difference between wood carving and whittling? The two main distinctions are apparent in the dictionary definitions of the two terms. To **whittle,** Webster's dictionary says, is "to pare or cut off chips from the surface of (wood) with a knife." But **wood carving,** it says, is "the art of fashioning or ornamenting objects of wood by cutting with a sharp implement." Thus, while whittling usually is limited to the use of a knife, wood carving is not, and wood carving is considered an art, while whittling is not.

As with any art, wood carving involves learning the basics of design and technique. Design is what you want to do; technique is how you do it. Another consideration in wood carving is your choice of material. The wood you plan to carve must be compatible with the design and suitable for the technique and tools you want to use. Once you learn the basics of design, technique, and material selection, you should become well-versed on wood carving safety before starting a project. At that point, you will be able to complete the Wood Carving merit badge requirements.

Carving Safely

Before you begin carving, be sure to consider safety issues. It's more fun to make a project when you think "safety first."

Wood carving involves the use of sharp carving tools such as knives. Taking safety seriously is important to avoiding injury and enjoying yourself as you carve. The Safety Checklist for Carving pinpoints five areas of importance in keeping safety first when carving:

- Personal maturity and judgment
- Caring for carving tools
- Controlling the work environment
- Handling knives
- Making the right choices

The Totin' Chip

Begin learning the basics of safety for wood carving by completing the requirements for the Totin' Chip. Boy Scouts earn the Totin' Chip to get good, basic information on knife safety. The Totin' Chip is like a driver's license for carving. You need it at Scout activities and functions. Carry it with you or tape it inside your *Wood Carving* merit badge pamphlet.

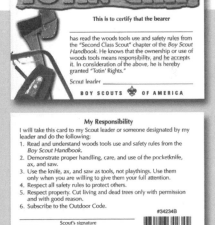

This is to certify that the bearer

has read the woods tools use and safety rules from the "Second Class Scout" chapter of the *Boy Scout Handbook*. He knows that the ownership or use of woods tools means responsibility, and he accepts it. In consideration of the above, he is hereby granted "Totin' Rights."

Scout leader _____

BOY SCOUTS OF AMERICA

My Responsibility

I will take this card to my Scout leader or someone designated by my leader and do the following:

1. Read and understand woods tools use and safety rules from the *Boy Scout Handbook*.
2. Demonstrate proper handling, care, and use of the pocketknife, ax, and saw.
3. Use the knife, ax, and saw as tools, not playthings. Use them only when you are willing to give them your full attention.
4. Respect all safety rules to protect others.
5. Respect property. Cut living and dead trees only with permission and with good reason.
6. Subscribe to the Outdoor Code.

#34234B

_____ Scout's signature

34234B
2001 Boy Scouts of America

7 30176 34234 4

Personal Maturity and Judgment

Knives and other carving tools are not toys—they can be very dangerous if not used properly. Discuss with your parents when and where you may carve while at home.

Owning or handling a knife comes with certain responsibilities. Never bring a knife or carving tools to school without permission. In most cases, this is illegal. Horseplay is not funny, either. Engaging in horseplay will cause you to lose the privilege of using knives until you are more mature. In addition, never throw carving tools and other knives. Not only is this hard on the tools, but more importantly you could injure others or damage property.

You also should exercise good judgment while at the carving table. Too much visiting while you are carving can distract you. If you need to take a break, stop and move away from the carving area and continue your visiting in another place so you don't disturb other carvers. Also, remember that accidents are more likely to occur when you are tired. If you are tired, or if you are losing attention and are not alert, stop and rest.

Caring for Your Tools

Sharp is safe; dull is dangerous. There is no more important wood-carving safety rule than this, for safety is the result of using sharp tools and common sense. This applies whether you are talking about a pocketknife, gouge, or ax. Any dull cutting edge will skid off a piece of wood, but it will have no difficulty at all digging into your flesh. Keeping knives sharp is efficient, because the time you spend sharpening will easily save time by allowing you to cut faster and more accurately, as well as safely.

Proper care of tools and knives requires a few basic maintenance steps:

- Remember that tools are not toys and should not be treated as such.

- Keep tools sharp and free from rust and dirt.

- Always store tools in a safe place and away from children.

- Never use a knife as a screwdriver or as a lever to pry something open.

If you are old enough to use power tools, visit with a parent or shop teacher about proper use and safety procedures. When using hand tools or power tools, wear safety glasses to protect your eyes and a dust mask to keep from inhaling sawdust, especially if cutting out multiple pieces.

Remember:

Sharp is safe;

dull is dangerous.

Controlling Your Work Environment

Just as important as maintaining the integrity of the tools is keeping the work area conducive to wood carving. An ideal carving station includes a safety table, an adequate light source, and a sturdy chair. Covering the table with plastic, cloth, or heavy paper can protect its surface. A plastic mat or bench stop can provide extra control and safety. Keep a clean work surface so debris or tools don't get in your way.

When choosing a place to locate a carving table, pick one that has enough space so that no one is in danger of bumping you. If you have difficulty seeing the details in the carving, your light source may not be good enough. Get more light or move the carving area.

Equip your carving station with a clamp or bench stop to use for control when carving smaller or odd-shaped projects. Use a clamp to secure wood if you are cutting out your project by hand with a coping saw. As you carve, keeping your elbows on the table will provide more control so you will be less likely to get cut.

Handling Knives

Proper knife handling is important to keeping safe. Be sure to follow these guidelines whenever you handle any carving tool:

- Do not pass a knife across other people when sitting at a table. Someone can jostle the knife from your hands, and it could land in your lap or another Scout's lap. The photo here shows the proper way to pass a knife to your neighbor.

- Always carve at a table—never in your lap. Carving in your lap poses physical danger if your knife slips or the wood cracks and your tool continues in the direction that you started it.

- Never carve near your face. If someone accidentally bumps into you, you could be seriously injured.

- Avoid taking long strokes as you carve. Taking small, well-placed carving strokes gives you more security and control. Using long strokes makes carving more dangerous and may mess up your project. Carefully place each stroke so that every cut contributes to the desired look of the piece.

- Never "muscle" a project when carving. If you find yourself working hard to get a knife to cut through wood, you are either trying to cut off too much wood or the knife blade is dull. Trying to force the knife could result in injury if the knife slips. Also, never hammer the top of a knife to make a cut.

- Be sure to close the knife carefully when you are finished carving, as shown here.

Making the Right Choices

You have several decisions to make before beginning a project. After you decide what your finished work will be, you must choose the appropriate type of wood, considering the desired qualities such as color, hardness, and grain.

When selecting a project to carve, don't try to carve a project that exceeds your ability. Start with the simple objects until your technique is good.

Safety Checklist for Carving*

Sit down with your parents and review this safety checklist to help make good safety rules at home.

1. Personal Maturity and Judgment

☐ Knives and other carving tools are not toys and should never be thrown.

☐ At home, carve only with your parent's approval.

☐ Carve only when you can focus on your work and are alert, and limit visiting while carving.

☐ Never bring a knife to school without permission.

☐ Never engage in horseplay around knives.

2. Caring for Your Tools

☐ Keep your tools and knives sharp and free from rust and dirt.

☐ If you are old enough to use power tools, make sure you understand how to use them properly.

☐ Wear protective gear such as safety glasses and, when appropriate, a dust mask.

☐ Store tools in a safe place and away from children.

☐ Never use a knife to pry something open.

3. Controlling the Work Environment

- [ ] Use a clamp or bench stop for better control when carving small or oddly shaped objects; use a plastic mat or bench stop for extra control and safety.
- [ ] Use a clamp to hold down wood when using a coping saw.
- [ ] Use a safety table with a sturdy chair and adequate lighting.
- [ ] Cover the table to protect its surface; keep adequate space around you with no one else close enough to bump you.
- [ ] Keep your elbows on the table for more control so you will be less likely to get cut.

4. Handling Knives

- [ ] Never pass a knife across other people at the table.
- [ ] Never carve in your lap or near your face.
- [ ] Take small, well-placed carving strokes that give you more control over your work.
- [ ] Never "muscle" a project when carving.
- [ ] Always make sure your knife is sharp. Dull knives are dangerous knives.
- [ ] Never hammer the top of a knife to make a cut.

5. Making the Right Choices

- [ ] Choose the right wood for the project.
- [ ] Start with simple projects.
- [ ] When laying out projects, have plenty of space for cutting them out.

---

* Reprinted with permission from the author, Jeff Springer, Topeka, Kansas.

First Aid

Prevention is the best way to avoid cuts, nicks, and other injuries. Use the preventive measures discussed in the Safety Checklist for Carving and in the *Boy Scout Handbook,* and you should have a safe and enjoyable experience with wood carving.

However, as a Scout working with wood and knives, you should be prepared in the event of a cut or perhaps a splinter. If you are injured, stay calm and let the adult in charge know what has happened.

Treating Minor Cuts

Sometimes accidents happen even when all safety precautions are taken. For a serious cut or gash, seek medical help immediately. For minor cuts and scrapes, follow these first aid steps:

Step 1—Stop the bleeding by applying pressure with a clean, absorbent cloth; if cloth is unavailable, use your fingers.

Step 2—If the blood soaks through, apply a second bandage on top. Do not take off the first bandage because that will disturb the clotting that has already taken place.

Step 3—If bleeding still does not stop, raise the wound above the victim's heart level.

Step 4—Once the bleeding has stopped, clean the wound gently with soap and water, or just water. It is very important to remove all debris and dirt.

Step 5—Apply an antibiotic ointment. Remember, some people are allergic to these ointments, so contact your doctor if you have any doubts.

Removing Splinters

You can usually remove a splinter easily with tweezers and a steady hand. If the thought makes you uncomfortable, ask an adult for help. Remember to wash the area with soap and water both before and after removing the splinter.

Step 1—Sterilize a needle or tweezers by passing the end over a flame. Let the needle cool before using it.

Step 2—If the splinter is sticking out from the skin, grasp the protruding end and pull it out at the same angle that it entered. If it is just under the skin, gently loosen the skin around the splinter with the sterile needle and remove it with tweezers. You can also try using ordinary transparent tape to gently remove the splinter.

Step 3—If a splinter is close to the surface and cannot be removed gently with tweezers, try rubbing a pumice stone along the direction of the splinter. If this fails, speak with an adult. You may need to see a doctor to prevent infection.

Know Your Woods

Picking the right wood can greatly enhance the look of a project. Most Scouts will not have the choice of many woods. The local lumber store usually carries a variety of woods for buildings and a few other types for hobbyists or furniture makers. If you must use something from the lumberyard, pick the softest piece with the least grain. Look for a straight grain with little discoloration and few knots.

Composition

Most wood comes from the stem, or trunk, of a tree. The stem supports the crown, or limbs and leaves, and must be very strong. It also must be elastic to withstand wind pressure. The stem carries nutrients from the roots to the leaves, which make food for the tree and carry it back to the roots.

The ideal structure for this complex system would be a series of layers surrounding a tough, flexible, solid core. A tree trunk is like that. To grow, the tree adds new layers around the old ones each year from the inside, beneath the protective bark. It forms what are known as **annual rings,** visible in a cross-section of a tree trunk— for instance, a stump or the end of a plank. As growth begins in early spring, the new cells are large and soft, but as the summer gets hotter and drier, the new cells get smaller, harder, and closer together.

Summerwood (the part of the annual ring that develops late in the growing season) is harder and less porous than **springwood**. Summerwood can be distinguished from springwood because it tends to be much darker. However, in birch, maple, gum, and some pine woods, the distinction is hard to see.

The thickness of the annual ring depends on how much the tree grew during the year. The appearance and hardness of the wood depends on the individual tree's growing conditions as well as on the characteristics of that kind of tree.

Seasoning

Another quality of wood that directly affects your work is dryness. **Seasoning** wood gives it more stability. If wood is seasoned, you can be more certain that it will maintain its shape after it is carved and that it will not split or warp.

Most lumber is air-dried; that is, after it has been cut into planks or timbers, it is left out to dry for as long as several years. Much of the moisture in the wood evaporates quickly. This type of drying is less desirable because it leaves the lumber still able to absorb moisture from the air and therefore prone to warping.

The preferred method of seasoning is kiln drying. In kiln drying, most of the sap and water is forced out of the lumber by heating the wood in an oven. This seems to shrink the fibers so that they do not absorb the air's moisture as readily; thus, the wood is not liable to warp or split. Kiln-dried wood is expensive but, for many uses, worth the cost.

Hardwood or Softwood?

The terms "hardwood" and "softwood" have little to do with hardness. In fact, some softwoods are much harder than some hardwoods. **Hardwood** is a forester's term for a tree with broad leaves that fall each year. **Softwoods** are trees that have narrow leaves or needles and bear seed cones. The many differences between hardwoods and softwoods are of relatively little importance to the wood carver.

Grain of hardwood

Favorite Carving Woods

As you may expect, different types of woods are valuable for the different qualities they exhibit in a finished piece. You may choose a wood for its color, grain, strength, texture, or ease of carving, or for a combination of many of its qualities.

White Pine

Pine ranges in color from creamy white to yellow, tan, or pink, with occasional blue stain imperfections. There is almost no figure to the grain no matter how it is cut, and these is only a slight difference between springwood and summerwood. Pine usually is straight-grained and even-textured. Small details might chip off if worked with dull tools.

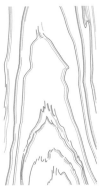

Grain of softwood

For whittling and some carving projects, eastern white pine is best. For the small quantity needed, even the best grades will be relatively inexpensive. You might even find just the piece you need between the knots in the less costly grades.

However, the choicest pieces of white pine might not be available. You may have to settle for sugar pine, which is nearly as good as the eastern white pine. More alternative choices include ponderosa pine and Idaho white pine.

Butternut

Butternut is yellowish and soft. Wood carvers who use this wood must be careful not to overcut.

Oak

American white oak and red oak may be used for carving. White oak is strong, very hard, and light in color, and it has a fairly close grain. Red oak is softer, darker in color, and more likely to splinter. Because of its hardness, however, oak is not the best choice for the beginner.

Red Oak

Yellow Poplar (Tulip Tree)

Sometimes called whitewood, poplar is light, fine-textured, and easy to work. The sapwood is white and thick, but the heartwood can be yellow, green, olive, or brown—often with purple, blue, or black streaks. Its annual rings are distinct. The cucumber tree, actually a magnolia, is also called yellow poplar and has similar characteristics.

Basswood (Linden)

Basswood is a hardwood but is about as soft and work-able as white pine. Because it is straight-grained and even-textured, basswood makes an excellent wood for whittlers and beginning carvers. Basswood has no pro-nounced grain or color variations. It has a yellowish, medium-light color.

Mahogany

A hardwood, mahogany is a noble wood for carvers because of its beautiful color, its texture and grain, and its ability to take a fine polish. Honduran and Cuban mahoganies are best but are hard to get. Santo Domingo mahogany is good, but the Mexican, Philippine, and African varieties are not too suitable for carving.

Mahogany

Walnut

American or black walnut is similar to mahogany but usually is a yellowish brown color rather than red. A fine carving wood, walnut is often used for gun stocks, which are wood sculptures in themselves and often ornamented with delicate carvings. Walnut is quite hard, but not enough to dull tools too quickly. Walnut usually has an interesting surface pattern and is effective with a high polish.

American Walnut

Black Cherry

Black and wild cherry are widely available in the

Black Cherry

eastern United States, often as weed trees. You might be able to get bolts of this wood from a farm woodlot. Both types of cherry are available commercially, but they might be hard to find.

Cherry wood ranges from a light to dark reddish brown. The sapwood is very light but also rather narrow. A rare and beautiful native cabinet wood, cherry is easy to carve, having an even texture and close grain. There is enough difference between the summerwood and spring-wood to show a figure, but not enough to make a big difference. Cherry must be seasoned slowly to avoid splitting.

Sweetgum

The durable, even-textured heartwood of the sweetgum tree is known as red gum. Occasional dark streaks make it resemble a figured walnut. Sweetgum lacks very distinct annual rings, but its **radial lines** show up well in quarter-sawed stock. This feature and the red color have led some to call it "American mahogany." Sweetgum is easy to work and takes a wide variety of finishes. It is widely used for furniture.

Choosing a Type of Wood

As a wood carver, you will care about how easily an object can be carved, its appearance, and whether it will stand up under use. Many other factors play a role in your choice of wood. When choosing a type of wood for a project, ask yourself the following questions:

1. *How much will I spend on the project?* The monetary restraints will help you determine the type of wood and finish.

2. *Do I want to paint or stain the project?* If you chose walnut, for example, you would choose to stain the wood to show off the grain and color of the natural walnut.

3. *Has the wood been seasoned?* It is important to use wood that has been seasoned because it is more stable and less likely to warp.

4. *Will I use saws to cut out my project, or will I use blanks or roughouts?* Scouts may use **blanks** or **roughouts** that have already been sawn out for carving so that they do not have to cut out the project, which can be much safer than using hand saws or power saws. Many wood carvers use blanks or roughouts because they have no way to cut out their project and the wood is usually of a better quality than is found in lumberyards. (Most blanks are of basswood, sugar pine, or butternut hickory.)

You may think a blank is expensive, but by the time you go to the lumberyard, buy lumber by the board foot, and get someone to cut out or help you cut out your project, you may have a lot more invested than you think. Whenever possible, a Scout should find out the type wood in his blank and why it was laid out and cut the way it was. Consider the direction of the grain, for instance.

If you decide to cut out your project, keep this in mind: Lay out projects so they are not so close together they are difficult to saw out. Also, a good layout on your block of wood may save you wood so you could have enough left for a second project.

5. *How dense is the wood?* The more dense wood is, the heavier it is. Oak, walnut, maple, and ash are heavy woods. These woods are beautiful for the right project but carving them proves to be very hard on tools. These woods are usually found in furniture or projects turned on a lathe. They can be carved, but the wood carver should be prepared to resharpen the tools often.

6. *Is the wood winter cut?* The better carving woods are usually winter cut because trees don't have as much sap in the winter. When wood is put in a drying kiln, any sap in the wood becomes a hard yellow rosin that is very difficult to put a knife through. Because winter-cut wood has less sap, it will be easier to carve.

7. *Is the board fairly straight?* You can look down the edge of the wood to see if the board is fairly straight or if it is warped. If you are using small pieces, this may not be important. If the board is not straight, it could later twist, ruining the project with cracks and splits.

8. *Are the annual rings regularly spaced and even?* If you look at the cross-cut end of a piece of wood, you may see one of two things: First, the wood may have two sets of curves facing opposite directions. Second, you may see a large space between the annual rings where the cell development, called **pith,** could be weak. When you try to carve pith, it will not hold up to the pressure you are using and that area may actually crush. Either of these conditions can cause difficulty in carving.

9. *What woods are available in my area?* You may have to use a lower-quality wood because that's what is available.

10. *What if I want to get the wood for my project from a tree?* Use wood that has already been cut or that has fallen naturally from the tree, such as after a windy thunderstorm. If everyone cut down trees for their projects, we could not enjoy the beauty of the outdoors.

11. *Am I making a walking stick?* When picking a limb or stick to carve a walking stick, you would be smart to let it dry out—season—for four to six months. This will help reduce cracking. If the walking stick has many knots in it where limbs once protruded, this is usually where cracking might occur. Remember that it may be fun to have the walking stick now to use, but if you let it dry you are more likely to have a beauty for years to come.

If you need to make one now, you may want to leave 6 inches or more on the top and bottom of the walking stick so if it cracks while drying, you could cut the extra length off.

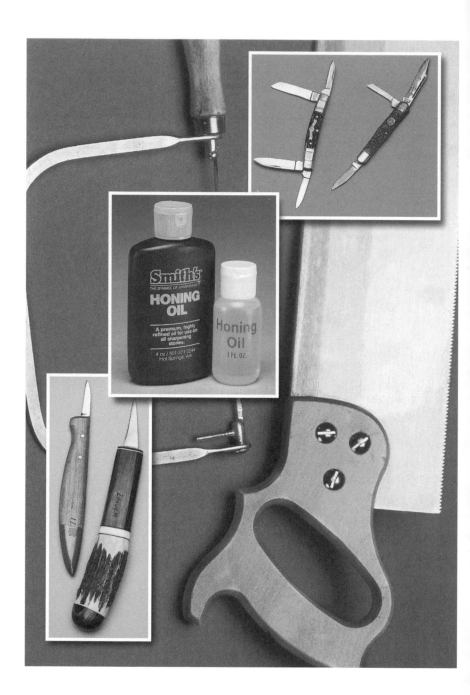

Know Your Tools

Before beginning to work with wood, you should know the basic types of tools and how to keep them in top condition, including how to keep knives sharp. You also should pay special attention to creating a work area that will keep you safe and help you concentrate. The first step in learning about tools is picking a pocketknife that is right for you.

Pocketknives

There are many types of pocketknives. For carving, your best bet is the **whittler's knife,** which has three blades. The Scout whittler's knife is a good beginner's knife. The largest blade on the whittler's knife is an all-purpose blade, sometimes called a **master blade.**

The blade with a flat carving edge is called a **sheep-foot blade.** This blade is sometimes used as a coping blade when cutting away the outside or profile, to remove wood that is not needed. Some carvers will use this blade for most of their project.

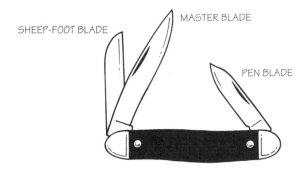

SHEEP-FOOT BLADE

MASTER BLADE

PEN BLADE

The third blade on this knife is a **pen blade.** Many people use this for carving details like eyes and other facial features. Be sure not to use a stockman's knife. It looks similar to the whittler's knife, but the blade is too flat to use as a pen blade.

The **congress knife** has four blades. This is a good knife to use because it usually has two pen blades on it. If one blade gets dull, you can use the extra pen blade until you have a chance to resharpen. The congress knife also has a sheep-foot blade. These two blades (the pen and sheep foot) are the most commonly used blades in wood carving. The fourth blade is usually an all-purpose or master blade that can be used for carving bark, cutting rope, or other cutting chores at the campsite.

Do more delicate finishing on curved or other surfaces with a small wood-carver's knife. This tool should be used only when the carving has been finished as much as possible with the chisel. Depending on the effect desired, either the whole or the parts of a finished carving are smoothed first with medium, then with fine, sandpaper. Delicate details should not be sanded at all.

Before carving a project, practice using tools on a piece of waste wood or on the backside of the project. You can use a cut stop, score the line, then carve back to the line with the gouge. This will help you practice making pieces of wood fall out in the places that you desire.

Other Carving Tools

You probably will want to use more tools than a pocketknife to complete a wood-carving project, but don't buy a set of carving tools with more than five tools. You probably will never use all of them. You may want to start with a straight carving knife, any V-tool, and a straight gouge. You can buy more tools as you determine that you need them.

Carving tools come in two types: straight-handled and palm tools. Many new carvers find palm tools easy to grasp and use. Carving tools also come in different cutting edges, like V-tools and gouges.

Craft knives

Straight carving knives

V-tool, ¼-inch; straight gouge, ¼-inch

Whittler's knives with carving blade

Vises or clamps for safety, to keep your project in place

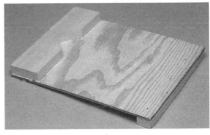

Bench stop, for stability

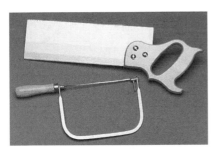

Back saw, *top,* for cutting wood in straight cuts only
Coping saw, *bottom,* good for cutting angles and curves

Thumb guard (or quilter's thumb), available at most sewing stores (Most carving supply stores have wood carver's safety gloves.)

Also consider other tools you may use with your project, such as rulers, pencils, clamps, vises, bench stops, and rubber mats. Experience will teach you how useful these items can be.

A carver also needs:

• A wooden mallet

• A flat wood file

• Medium and fine sandpaper

• Oil stones

• Slips for sharpening chisels and fine tools

The mallet is used when more force is needed on the chisel and when this force can be applied by hand. The flat wood file is used to remove irregularities and departures from the correct outline on workpieces.

Arranging the Work Space

It's very important that you use a steady table and chair and be sure you have a good light source so you can see what you are doing. The table or workbench should be away from distractions so you can concentrate.

Care of Tools

While you don't need your own tools to earn this merit badge, you should have a general knowledge of caring for and sharpening the tools you use. Most knives must be sharpened before use, and doing a good job could take a couple of hours.

Check tools for dirt and rust on a regular basis. A pocketknife that you carry in your pocket may also pick up lint. Use a light coat of honing oil and let it set for awhile. Then wipe off the excess oil before using.

Keep tools in the best possible condition by making sure they are dry. Wipe off fingerprint marks and moisture with a dry cloth. Apply a couple of drops of oil to the blades and joints of a knife. Keep chisels, gouges, and other tools wrapped in a soft cloth so they do not damage each other while stored.

When Is a Tool Sharp?

Before sharpening knives and tools, check first to see if they need sharpening. Stand facing the sun or any strong source of light, holding the knife or tool with the cutting edge upward. Hold the tool in front of your body at about chest height. Any reflection from the light on the cutting edge of the tool will indicate a dull spot that requires sharpening.

The safest way to test the sharpness of an edge is to use it on a piece of wood that is similar to the wood in the project you will be carving. Practice some simple cuts on a block of wood. This should tell you whether the knife needs to be sharpened.

Most knives do not come presharpened for wood carving. Blades usually come with an all-purpose edge since the manufacturer does not know how you will use the knife. Some knives may have a utility edge, which lasts longer, especially if you are using it on rope or the bark on a tree limb. Both of these are hard on a very sharp knife.

The Carving Edge

Your knife will need a carving edge. Putting a carving edge or wire edge on a knife takes away some of the extra metal from the blade. This will make it thinner (and easier) for passing through your wood.

To achieve a carving edge on your knife, you will need a sharpening stone kit, which most discount stores and sporting goods stores sell. Some of the sharpening stone kits come with two stones, a large stone and a small stone. The large stone is the first stone you would use to get the blade shaped the way you want it—in this case, a carving edge. Then it is time to use the smaller stone, which is the honing stone.

Sharpening Stones

It is important to learn how to use any sharpening stone the right way. There are a number of sharpening stones on the market:

- **Silicon carbide, or crystolon:** Blue-black in color, available in coarse, medium, and fine grits. Also available in sheet abrasives. Used with oil.

- **Aluminum oxide, or India:** Usually reddish-brown, but can be gray or white. Available in coarse, medium, and fine grits. Synthetic sapphires are aluminum oxide. Used with oil.

- **Arkansas, or novaculite:** A natural stone (which can be almost pure silicon) ranging in color from white to black, and mined in Arkansas. The stone's hardness does not depend on color. Available in coarse, medium, and fine grits. Most carvers use oil on this stone, but some prefer water.

- **Ouachita:** Similar to Arkansas but coarser. Mined near the Ouachita River in Arkansas. Used with water.

- **Japanese water stones:** Can be either natural or synthetic. Available in grits from coarse to very fine. The fine polishing stones, called *shiage toishi,* contain a polishing compound. Stones must be soaked in water five to 10 minutes before use.

- **Nagura:** Synthetic stone from Japan. Nagura is rubbed in a circular motion over a wet stone to reduce the abrasive to a paste consistency, which saves time and encourages even wear on the stone.

- **Ceramic:** Synthetic, from aluminum oxide. Used dry, but must be washed often with water, a dish pad, and a household cleaner. This new stone is highly praised by wood carvers.

- **Diamond:** Fine monocrystalline diamond particles are permanently fixed to a flat plastic base in a screen pattern. Water is used as a lubricating wash. This stone is cleaned with soap and water. You can use a diamond stone to flatten worn Arkansas and Japanese stones.

HONING OIL

Using honing oil helps preserve the original quality of the stones by filling their surface pores and washing away metal particles during the sharpening process. Some wood carvers use either oil or water on Arkansas and Ouachita stones.

Honing oil can be made using a mixture of half 30-weight oil and half kerosene. Do not use an oil-impacted stone. These are for use with larger tools such as axes and carpenter's chisels, not for fine wood-carving tools.

Care of Stones

New stones that are going to be used with oil should first be lightly oiled, wrapped in aluminum foil, and stored until the stone is completely saturated. Storage boxes are essential to keep the stones from drying and free from dust and dirt. Stones can be resurfaced with a diamond stone or, if they are not too badly worn, by rubbing them over emery cloth or silicon carbide paper. Carborundum powder spread on a piece of plate glass or cast iron also works well. Use water as a lubricating wash during this process.

Always use oil or water on stone. Most stones require oil, but always follow the manufacturer's instructions. Water or oil will prevent heat from building up in the blade you are sharpening. If you get the blade too hot, it can take out some of the carbon and it will no longer keep a sharp edge. (This is why you should never put a knife in the dishwasher.)

Never use an electric grindstone on carving tools. The speed of the wheel can burn up the carbon in the steel, making the tool nearly worthless. If you are using a buffing wheel or leather wheel, the same thing can happen. Also, pushing a tool into the wheel can actually dull a tool.

After you have finished sharpening, clean the stone by lightly wiping off the excess oil. Do not use pressure, since the oil has picked up some of the metal filings. You don't want to fill the pores on the surface of the stone.

It's much safer to put the stone on the table instead of in your hands because if your blade goes past the end of the stone, your fingers may get in the way of the edge, resulting in cuts. For increased safety, you can make a cradle to hold your stone. Securing your cradle with a clamp or laying it on a rubberized shelf liner will keep it from sliding around.

Keeping little or no angle between your knife and the stone that is being used, move the blade, starting closest to the handle. The knife is always going down the stone like you were trying to carve or cut it. After using the coarse or medium stone, move to a finer stone.

The most important part of sharpening takes place when the knife is almost done. The edge will look sharp, but you will see small burrs on the opposite side of whichever side was on the stone last. Pull the knife through the end of a piece of wood to get rid of these burrs. Strap the knife on a slipstick or a leather strop. You must pull the knife back toward you on the strop. This will take off any burrs that were left from the stones.

Slipsticks and Leather Strops

A slipstick can be used in the same way as a sharpening stone. Start by using paint mixing sticks that are new and flat, or any flat stick of a similar size. Glue a piece of rubber (such as from an inner tube) across the top. Then glue a medium-grade emery paper to one stick and a finer emery paper to another. For honing, attach a piece of leather to the slipstick; this will give your blade a razor-sharp edge. Remember, you need to strap a slipstick just as you do when using sharpening stones.

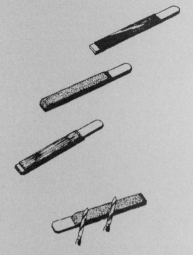

Leather strops are made the same as slipsticks, but on a piece of hardwood. A strop made with leather on both sides will enable various honing grits to be used. Silicon carbide in 240 and 600 grit, with a little oil, is used to charge the leather. Some experts prefer chromium oxide as a honing compound. You might wish to make a stick covered with smooth hard leather, dressed with real soap. Do not allow your fingers to touch the surfaces of the strops.

Basic Cuts

In wood carving, there are five cuts that you are most likely to use:

- Paring cut
- Basic cut
- Score line
- Stop cut
- V-cut

When practicing making these cuts, remember to keep your elbows on the table as much as possible. This keeps you from taking long, dangerous strokes. Take your time and make short, shallow cuts.

Paring Cut

Take very small cuts toward you. This enables you to get into spaces that another stroke cannot. (Note the thumb guard the Scout is wearing to protect himself.)

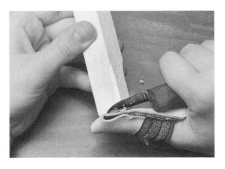 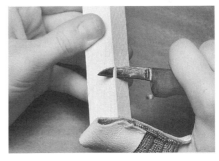

Basic Cut

This cut is also known as the push cut. This cut is away from you, taking small pieces of wood. By placing the opposite thumb on the

back of the blade, you are creating a lever and making it easier to remove the wood from your project.

Score Line

This cut gives you a line that you can cut back to, to make a clear line or feature.

Stop Cut

This cut is used mostly with scoring a line. You will cut back to the line that you have scored. Most of the time, small pieces of wood will fall out. You can also use this when using gouges.

V-Cut

You can make a V-cut either with a knife or with a V-tool.
To use a knife, you will make three cuts:

1. Hold the knife straight up and down and score a line.

2. Put the knife in a pencil grip at a similar angle you would use to write. A right-handed person, for example, would do this on the right of the first cut. Remove wood in a wedge shape down to the original cut.

3. When possible, turn the wood around to make a similar cut on the other side. Or, repeat the cut on the left side.

Using a V-tool involves fewer steps:

1. Make a little cut stop at the place where you want the V-cut to end.

2. Guide the tool down to the cut stop, making the V cut.

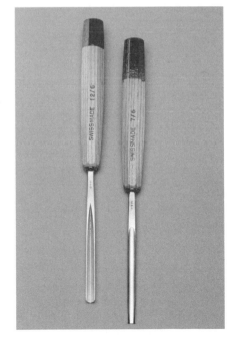

Carving in the Round

Making a three-dimensional carving is known as carving in the round. These carvings include neckerchief slides, small statues, and walking sticks. A slide does not have to be carved on the back side.

Considerations When Choosing a Project

You may already know what you want to carve. But if you do not, this section describes a few projects that you might like to try. (You may also want to check the slides featured in the *Boys' Life* "Slide of the Month" articles.)

Precut blanks are a convenient option. But make sure you pick out something that matches your ability and is not just something that looks cool. For instance, it may take you years to develop enough skill to carve faces.

Also, keep your project small; this will help keep the cost low.

Before Beginning a Project

Once you have a project in mind, you may want to first practice on a piece of scrap wood. If you are a real beginner, you may get a good plastic picnic knife and practice your cuts or designs on an apple. This can be fun because the apple will shrink when it dries and may look interesting the next day. It is very safe, because the tools will not have to be very sharp.

The best projects are planned and thought through before carving begins. Look at parts of the project to see what is closer to you and what's farther away. If you are doing a side view, features such as a hat and an ear

All slides need a back. Cut a small piece of plastic plumbing pipe with a ⅝-inch to ¾-inch inside hole. Glue this to the back of the slide using panel construction adhesive. Or, take a small piece of wood, drilling a hole ⅝ inch to ¾ inch. Repeat this on all sides needing backs. After the glue dries, it may be easier to hold onto when you paint your slide.

would be closer, while a nose would be farther back. Many wood carvers will draw out on paper and sometimes in perspective, to get a picture in their mind before taking a knife to their project.

Before cutting the project, be sure to lay it out using the grain to make it strong. For example, if your project were a carving of a dog, you would lay out your design so that the grain follows the same direction as a leg.

Before you start your first in-the-round project, review the following for safety and better results:

- Draw the design as carefully and accurately as possible. Many young carvers will pick projects much too hard for a beginner. The more complicated the drawing on the slide, the more difficult it usually is to carve.

- Check that all tools needed for the project are sharp and ready to use.

- Review the five types of cuts used in wood carving.

- Check the work area for lighting, clamps, and vises as needed. Make sure you have a sturdy work table.

You can ask for help from your counselor, Scout leader, or parent.

Finishing a Wood Carving Project

Most of the time, a carver does not sand a project. The carver will want it to look like the hand-carved project it is, not like a piece of store-bought plastic.

After carving the project, you may want to paint or stain it. *It is not a requirement of this merit badge to do so.* However, it will make a carving last many more years, and a good paint job can make it look better. Don't use too many colors, because it can overwhelm the workmanship.

You can make small changes from an original design that will make it appear different. Examples would be such things as changing the eyes, using different hats, and adding features such as a mustache on a figure.

Any carving project can be picked apart and planned so you can do it step-by-step. Think about how you would carve it. This will make a project easier to do. Start off slowly, and have fun carving.

First Project: Practice Stick

This project is a practice stick that can help you learn how to use a knife.

Step 1—Get a piece of wood, ¾-by-¾-inch and 6 inches long.

Step 2—Come down the side of the stick ¾ inch, making a box on all four sides. Repeat this three to four times, creating ¾-inch squares down the stick. This will leave you a portion of the stick to hold onto.

Step 3—In the top box, draw the same design on all four sides of the stick. Pick a new shape and repeat this in the next square down, then all around the stick. Repeat again on the third set of drawn squares. (Shapes such as diamond, square, house, and other geometric designs work well.)

Step 4—Carve each individual box all the way around before going to the next box. This repetition will give you practice doing similar cuts over and over again.

Remember: The neater the layout, the easier it is to carve the project.

Projects to Try*

You may choose projects that are not in this pamphlet. But if you like, you may use one of these.

*The projects in this section are the property of Jeff Springer, Topeka, Kansas, and are reproduced here with his permission.

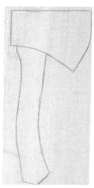

Step 1

The Ax Neckerchief Slide©

Step 1—Draw the ax onto a block of wood 5 inches with the grain and 2 3/8 inches across the grain. Use basswood if possible.

Step 2—Cut or carve the outside shape of the ax. Score the line between the handle and the head of the ax. Draw a line on the side of the handle and carve the entire handle down to the line without rounding the edge at this time.

Step 3—After carving the handle flat along the entire front view, round off the two front edges of the ax handle.

If the knife blade starts taking off more and more wood, stop and change the direction you are carving. You're probably hitting a grain change in the wood, or you're going into the wood at too much of an angle. Flatten the knife blade angle and take small, deliberate cuts.

You may be tempted to put a sharp edge on the ax, but it only has to be tapered. You can make it look like a sharp ax when you paint it.

Step 4—Glue on the slide back. Let the glue dry, and then paint. The handle has been left natural. Use medium gray (not silver) for most of the head. Add white to medium gray and paint in the sharpened area.

Step 2

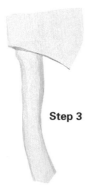

Step 3

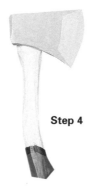

Step 4

The Eagle Neckerchief Slide©

Step 1—Transfer the eagle design onto a block of wood 3⅜ inches with the grain and 2¼ inches across the grain. Use basswood, if possible.

Step 2—Cut or carve out the outside profile of the eagle.

Step 3—Score the line separating the beak and forehead of the eagle. Then, carve back to your score line, keeping the beak flat at this time.

Step 4—Score the line separating the upper and lower parts off the beak. Carve on the lower part of the beak so it is recessed from the top. Now, you can round off and shape the top of the beak.

Step 5—Score the back part of the eagle head. Carve back and use a stop cut to the line that you have scored. Slightly round off the top and bottom of this back portion of the eagle head, making the top and bottom look like they go around the neck of the eagle.

Step 6—Slightly carve the top and bottom and edges on the middle portion of the eagle. To give it a nicer look, carve a little off near where the middle section meets the back part and the beak.

Step 7—Now, carve the details, including the eye and air vent hole.

Step 8—Glue on slide back. Let the glue dry and paint the slide. The eagle in the slide shown has a yellow beak, white middle, and brown end. The eye and vent hole on the beak are black.

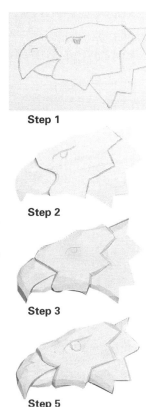

Step 1

Step 2

Step 3

Step 5

Step 8

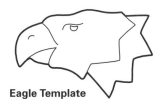

Eagle Template

Step 1

Step 2

Step 3

Step 5

Antelope Neckerchief Slide©

To carve an antelope slide, follow these directions, which are similar to the eagle slide directions:

Step 1—Draw the design on a block of wood (4¼-by-2¼ inches).

Step 2—Cut or carve the outside profile of the antelope.

Step 3—Score the line between the neck and jaw bone so you can use it as a cut stop when you are shaping the neck.

Step 4—Score a line below the ear and cut back to it, shaping the back portion of the neck.

Step 5—Score a line above the ear and reduce the antler.

Step 6—Using a combination of paring cut, basic cut, and push cut, shape the antler, the front side of the head, and the lower side of the head near the neck. (Remember, the lower part of the head will be slightly tapered into the nose.)

Step 7—To add details, score a line in the ear and stop cut back to it, indicating a lower area in the ear. Carve lines on the antler using V-cuts. Now, score lines and shape the eye, then undercut the mouth area. Take a little wood out of the nose area for a nostril.

Step 8—Glue on slide back. Let the glue dry and paint the slide. The slide as pictured is clear stained and the eye is painted black.

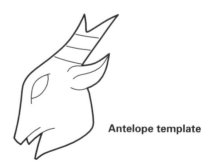

Antelope template

Step 8

Wizard or Saint Nick©

Use your imagination to give this little figure more personality by changing a few details here and there. By painting the figure in different color schemes, he can resemble a wizard or jolly ole Saint Nick.

Step 1—Carefully draw the slide view onto a piece of wood 4 inches tall, 2 inches wide, and 1⅝ inch thick. Then, draw the front view. Make sure you draw out this project accurately.

You can change things on this little man, such as having a foot stick out from his robe. Or, you could make his beard longer by adding a little on before cutting it out.

Step 1

Step 2—Cut the front view first, saving both pieces that you have cut away. Then, tape the cut pieces back together to reform the block as it was when you first started. After you tape it, set it on the side with the side view pencil lines showing, then cut out.

Pencil in a light center line on the front. This will help you center the nose, hat, and any changes you may have made from the project pictured. Use the knife to shape the hat.

Step 2

Step 3—Score in a pocket line on the front and back of the arms, then cut back to your score lines. This will make the arms pop out. Take a little off the arm. This will make the sleeve look as if it is going into the pocket. Repeat this on the other side. Cut a little on the back inside of both arms. At this time, you can rough out the hair on both sides of the figure. (Don't do individual hairs yet.)

Step 4—Cut around the nose. Leave it bigger than you need it. You may like a rounder St. Nick with big, jolly cheeks and nose. You can always take away more wood later.

Step 3

Step 4

Step 5

Step 6

Step 7

But once you take the wood off, it may be too late to have jolly cheeks and nose on this project. Take your time and make very small, deliberate cuts.

Step 5—Rough in the mustache, lower beard, and sideburns. Start shaping the nose.

Step 6—Make small cuts near the nose for the eyes in the figure. (See "Carving Eyes.")

Step 7—After carving St. Nick's eyes, paint the figure. Take your time and do a careful paint job. The St. Nick pictured has a red hat and robe. His face is light pink with red added to the pink to give him rosy cheeks. He has white hair.

Adding a splash of color helps bring the project to life.

Carving Eyes

If you have practiced making V-cuts with the knife or a V-tool, you are ready to carve an eye. Follow these steps:

Step 1—On both sides of the nose, cut a line across. These lines should be a few degrees lower on the outside edge. Take a second cut, carving from the top of where the eye will start, down to the lines. This will give you flat areas on which to carve the eyes later.

Step 2—Make the same cuts as you did in step 1, but from the bottom of the eye. Cuts may be slightly smaller.

Step 3—On the outside edge of the wedge cuts you made in steps 1 and 2, take a small gouge or knife and remove about ⅛ inch. (This is a good place to use a small gouge on the outside of each eye.)

Step 4—On top of this gouge mark, cut three or four tiny V-cuts. (This is on the outside of each eye to make little squint lines.)

Step 5—Take a pencil and draw the top of the eyelid. Do this for each eye. Deeply score the line that separates the top and lower wedges of each eye. Now, on both eyes, take a V-tool to cut an upside-down U that will touch each end of the scored line. This represents the upper part of the eyelid when closed.

Step 6—Carefully cut the line just above the eyelid line. This line will become the eyebrows. It's easy to break this off if you push too hard. Take a little of the wood away from above the eyebrow. Now, the eyebrows appear to be raised on the forehead.

Step 7—Using a V-tool or a knife, make V-cuts just below the center line you scored between the eye wedges earlier.

Step 8—Score a line just below and inside the upside-down U shape you carved in step 5. At this time, lay your knife as flat as you can and cut the corners out.

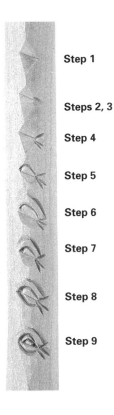

Step 1

Steps 2, 3

Step 4

Step 5

Step 6

Step 7

Step 8

Step 9

Step 9—Now, cut a little off between the two corners of the eye and below the line you scored in step 8. This gives you an eyeball. Repeat on the other side.

Walking Sticks

A walking stick can help when you are hiking over steep hills and uneven trails. Try your hand at this example, which features an eagle head as the hand grip.

Step 1—Looking down on the top end of the stick, turn the stick so the square becomes a diamond shape. Draw a straight line from the top of the diamond down to the bottom. Then draw two other parallel lines, both ³⁄₁₆ inch from each side of the center line.

Step 2—Keeping these lines vertical, make a small dot 9 inches down on one side edge of the stick. Repeat on the opposite edge.

Step 3—Draw a line connecting the left dot with the top of the left line you drew on the square. Then connect the dot with the bottom of the line. Do the same on the right.

Step 4—Taper the stick by carefully removing these outside corner wedges of wood from the dots forward. This will give a fairly flat surface on both sides to help you sketch the beak and head profile.

Step 5—Draw the eagle profile. Either sketch it on paper and transfer it to the flat surface of the wood, or draw it directly on the wood. To get the two eyes the same, draw and cut one eye on an index card. Use the card as a template and trace it on both sides of the head.

Step 6—Following the lines of the pattern, carve away wood from in front of the forehead and from the top and bottom of the beak.

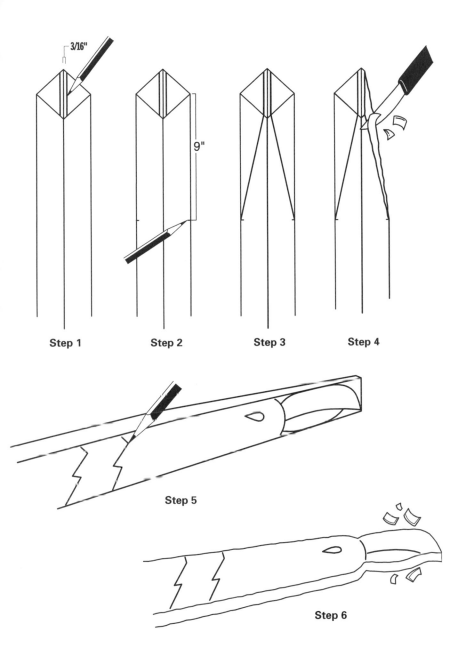

3/16"

9"

Step 1

Step 2

Step 3

Step 4

Step 5

Step 6

Step 7—At the back of the eagle's head, cut away the top and bottom edges of the stick. This will form the profile of the top feathers and will give you a complete silhouette of the eagle's head.

Step 8—Carve away wood from the sides of the beak, making it somewhat lower than the cheeks and slightly tapered toward the end. Remove a little extra wood from the sides of the bottom portion of the beak to make it appear the top part is coming down over it. Now soften the beak edges, rounding them out.

Step 9—Leaving the top and bottom edges of the head area alone, shape and round the sides to form the front part of the face, tapering it down to the beak.

Step 10—Score all the lines for feathers on one side of the eagle. (To score, hold the knife in a pencil grip, exerting force to make a cut ⅛ inch in depth. When a cut is made back to this line, it will act as a stop line and the piece of wood will fall out.) Starting with the layer farthest away from the beak, cut back to the score line to form the feathers. Repeat on the other side.

Step 11—Now that the eagle head is completely carved, round out the staff. Do not try to remove all the knife marks. The carvings will not only make the stick look more natural, they will also improve your grip. Round the edges of the bottom of the walking stick to help prevent cracking and chipping.

Step 12—Using oil or enamel, paint the eagle head. Paint the beak yellow, the eyes black, the back feathers brown, and the rest white. The staff itself should not be painted. After the paint is thoroughly dry, a coat of polyurethane, shellac, or varnish will help keep stains and dirt from discoloring the stick.

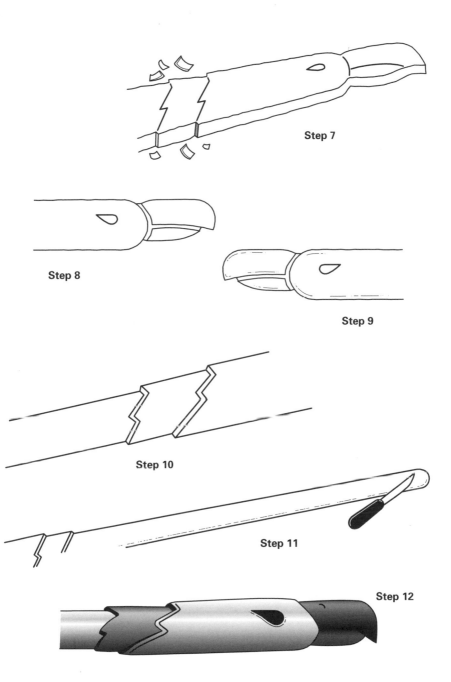

Step 7

Step 8

Step 9

Step 10

Step 11

Step 12

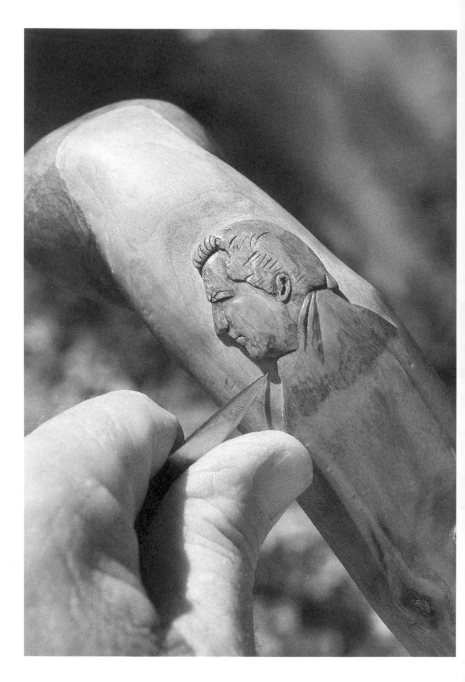

Relief Carving

Relief carving is a type of wood working in which the forms and figures seem to be raised out of the surface of the wood. Relief carving projects are usually done on a flat area, but you can also carve on rounded surfaces such as a walking stick.

To begin a relief carving project, make a simple line drawing. This may be cut with gouges, or a knife cutting away a wedge of wood, not just scratches or single cuts with a knife. Any of the five basic cuts can be used in relief carving, but the V-cut is the most efficient.

There is no set amount of wood to be taken off the project. Your counselor should be able to see that you have developed a plan and followed it. Keep the project to the level of your ability. If you try to get too fancy, you may just waste the wood.

As with knives, do not "muscle" gouges. You can hurt yourself or ruin the project. If the tool is not cutting, you may be taking off too much wood with the cut, or you may need to sharpen or touch up the edge of the tool.

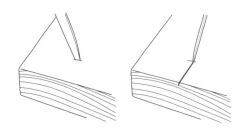

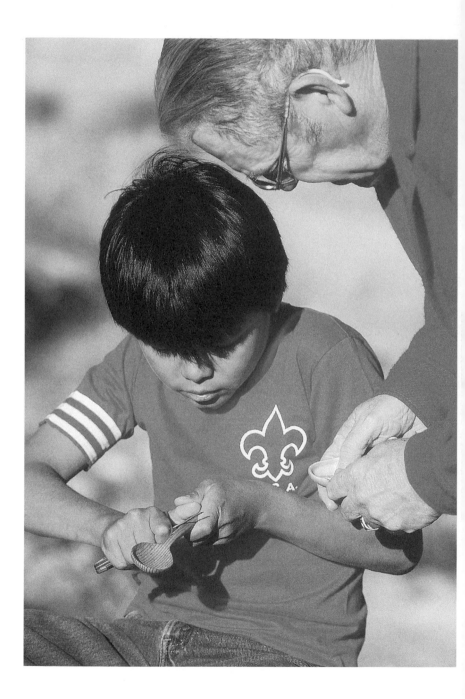

Glossary

annual rings. A layer of wood that is produced in a single year's growth, marked by springwood and summerwood.

blank. A piece of wood that is precut in the general shape of the desired finished piece.

congress knife. A pocketknife with four blades: usually two pen blades, one sheep-foot blade, and one all-purpose blade.

hardwood. A forester's term for a tree with broad leaves that fall each year. The many differences between hardwoods and softwoods are of relatively little importance to the wood carver.

master blade. The largest blade on the whittler's knife; an all-purpose blade.

pen blade. A blade on a pocketknife that usually is used for carving details like eyes and other facial features.

pith. Soft or spongy tissue that makes up part of a tree's annual growth. The pith is usually the light-colored band in a tree's annual growth ring.

radial lines. The lines of a tree's annual growth rings that are visible when the wood is quartered.

relief carving. The art of carving wood so that the figure looks to be raised from the wood base.

roughout. A piece of wood that is precut in the general shape of the desired finished piece.

seasoning. To prepare wood for use, usually by drying.

sheep-foot blade. The blade on a pocketknife that has a flat carving edge; sometimes used as a coping blade when cutting away the outside or profile, to remove wood that is not needed.

softwood. A tree that has narrow leaves or needles and bear seed cones. The many differences between hardwoods and softwoods are of relatively little importance to the wood carver.

springwood. The part of a tree's annual ring that develops early in the growing season.

summerwood. The part of a tree's annual ring that develops late in the growing season.

whittle. To use a knife to pare chips off a block of wood.

whittler's knife. A three blade pocketknife that is suitable for wood carving.

wood carving. The art of creating ornamental objects of wood by carving it with a sharp tool.

Resources

Books

Berry, P. *Start a Craft Wood Carving*. Book Sales, 1996.

Bridgewater, Alan. *Carving Totem Poles and Masks: Native American Folk Art*. Sterling, 1991.

Bridgewater, Alan. *Woodcarving Basics*. Sterling, 1996.

Green, Larry. *First Projects for Wood Carvers: A Pictorial Introduction to Wood Carving*. Schiffler, 1996.

Guldan, Mary D. *The Complete Beginner's Wood Carving Workbook: Ten Ready-to-Use Patterns*. Fox Chapel, 1996.

Tangerman, Elmer. *Carving Animals in Wood*. Dover, 1995.

Toney, Tina. *Easy Weekend Carving Projects: A Complete, Illustrated Manual*. Fox Chapel, 1996.

Tools and Supplies

If you have trouble finding supplies, try some of the places below. When you order, specify that you are a beginning wood carver so your project is not too difficult. All of the following businesses deal with carvers daily and can answer any question about wood carving tools and supplies.

Bob Reitmeyer, whittler—wood craft supplies for Scouts
Web site: *http://www.getasite.com/whittler.htm*
Source for neckerchief slide blanks.

Enlow Woodcarving
HCR 73 Box 95-C
Dogpatch, AR 72648
Telephone: 870-743-2671
Sells wood-carving blanks, tools, and books.

Falls Run Wood Carving Inc.
8105 Hawthorne Drive
Erie, PA 16509
Web site: *http://www.fallsrun.com*
Retailer of Flexcut® tools and knives.

Rossiter's Ruff-outs and Carving Supply
1447 South Santa Fe
Wichita, KS 67211
Telephone: 800-825-2657
Web site: *http://www.roughouts.com*
Source of wood-carving blanks and tools.

Woodcraft
Telephone: 800-225-1153
Web site: *http://www.woodcraft.com*
Retailer of wood as well as carving tools and books.

Acknowledgments

The Boy Scouts of America is indebted to devoted Scouter and master wood carver Jeff Springer of Topeka, Kansas, for his assistance with this edition of the *Wood Carving* merit badge pamphlet. The BSA thanks Mr. Springer for the use of his Safety Checklist for Carving and the plans reproduced in this book.

The BSA also gratefully acknowledges the assistance of the Circle Ten Council, Dallas, Texas, and the Jayhawk Area Council, Topeka, Kansas.

Notes

Notes

Notes

Notes